ASSARACUS

A Journal of Gay Poetry
Issue 1

Assaracus
A Journal of Gay Poetry
Issue 1: January 2011
ISBN 978-0-9832931-3-2
ISSN 2159-0478
Bryan Borland, Editor
Copyright © 2011 by Sibling Rivalry Press, LLC

All rights reserved. No part of this journal may be reproduced or republished without written consent from the publisher, except by reviewers who may quote brief excerpts in connection with a review in a newspaper, magazine, or electronic publication; nor may any part of this journal be reproduced, stored in a retrieval system, or transmitted in any form without written consent of the publisher. However, contributors maintain ownership rights of their individual poems and as such retain all rights to publish and republish their work. The cover photograph has been downloaded from the web, where it has been posted without source information. We presume copyright is retained by its owner. No infringement of copyright is intended.

Sibling Rivalry Press, LLC
13913 Magnolia Glen Drive
Alexander, AR 72002

www.siblingrivalrypress.com

ASSARACUS

Christopher Hennessy
p. 8

James Kangas
p. 17

Frank J Miles
p. 29

Eric Norris
p. 37

Raymond Luczak
p. 49

Jay Burodny
p. 62

Stephen Scott Mills
p. 74

Shane Allison
p. 88

Matthew Hittinger
p. 99

Gavin Dillard
p. 113

A NOTE FROM THE EDITOR

the comfortable familiarity of home

Assaracus (say it with me: Ass-UH-rack-us) came about after a drunken ménage à trois featuring *Mouth of the Dragon*, *Tribe*, and *Ganymede*. In truth, let's just call it conceived at a literary orgy, because Perry Brass and Gavin Dillard were there, too, with Perry sharing stories of a time when gay poetry was hot and forbidden, and handsome Gavin standing naked in the corner, reciting pieces from *A Day for a Lay: A Century of Gay Poetry*. And Vytautas Pliura was there, before he disappeared, leaving behind the smell of Illinois farm country and "Thomas," one of the most beautiful poems I've ever read. There was Uncle Walt. Auntie Allen. Cousin Harold and that ol' fag hag Sylvia Plath, who was bumming cigarettes before we kicked her out. This was a *men's* party, honey. At least on this occasion.

All of these people were in my head, dancing in iambic pentameter to the bottle of wine I'd downed, though even after I lost my buzz, I couldn't shake the exhilaration of what these publications—these poets and their poems—meant to me as a young gay man. Then I felt a responsibility, which brings us to these pages.

I know *Ganymede* is dead, what with the passing of John Stahle. *Mouth of the Dragon* and *Tribe* are no more. Forearm to forehead, I rescued a box containing a decade's worth of *Christopher Street* that was set to be burned by my local library.

True, we have Britain's *Chroma*, which recently announced a restructuring. We have *Gay and Lesbian Review-Worldwide*, but that publication serves another (necessary) purpose. Then there's *Mary: A Literary Quarterly*, which gives us a welcome taste of everything. But what I want to put into the world, because I yearn for it, because I think we need it, is a place for our poetry to dance with its own kind, to stand independently as a genre, just the words on the page and us, gay men, passing the book to our friends. No e-version. No iPhone. Just our fingers touching as we exchange a moment of electricity, a documentation of how we live, a love song through verse, a kinky couplet, a vivid memory, a night of sex with a stranger, and the morning after, when we return to the comfortable familiarity of home.

Why the name? It's a tribute to John Stahle, who first published me in *Ganymede*. Ganymede, of course, was the youth swept up by an eagle to serve Zeus. Assaracus was his earth-bound brother. Like it or not, we're earth-bound, but poetry can lift us to the heavens.

Assaracus has no formula. This quarterly journal will not contain a particular kind of poetry, only that the poems are authored by gay men. We're starting off with a bang, too, with Christopher Hennessey, James Kangas, Frank J (no period) Miles, Eric Norris, Raymond Luczak, Jay Burodny, Stephen Scott Mills, Shane Allison, Matthew Hittinger, and the previously-mentioned, Gavin Dillard, who this time is (mostly) clothed. These poets have very little in common, except that they are gay, and that their poems represent a vast spectrum of the talent within our community. I'd like to thank each one of these men for taking a chance on a yet unseen publication. I would like to especially thank Jay Burodny, who appears in print for the very first time with this issue. He's our first *John Stahle Discovery*, a young poet who deserves a microphone and a spotlight.

I hope *Assaracus* does these poets justice. Their work deserves to be read, and I hope our readers will want more than a one-night stand with these men. Seek out more work from them. Buy their books. Attend their readings. Write your phone numbers on their cocktail napkins. I hope *Assaracus* inspires more literary orgies. After all, we may be earth-bound, but our poetry is not.

Welcome to *Assaracus*.

- Bryan Borland

HENNESSY
CHRISTOPHER

just throw it like a man

Christopher Hennessy is the author of *Outside the Lines: Talking with Contemporary Gay Poets* (University of Michigan Press). He is a Ph.D. candidate in English Literature at the University of Massachusetts-Amherst. His poetry appeared in the *Ploughshares'* special "Emerging Writers" edition and his first book manuscript, *Love in Idleness*, was a finalist for the Four Way Books Intro Prize. His poetry, interviews, essays, and book reviews have appeared or are forthcoming in *American Poetry Review, Verse, Ploughshares, Cimarron Review, Court Green, The Writer's Chronicle, Bloomsbury Review, Crab Orchard Review, Natural Bridge, Wisconsin Review, Brooklyn Review*, and anthologies of gay poets and poets of social justice. Hennessy is an associate editor for the *Gay and Lesbian Review-Worldwide*. His first book of poetry is forthcoming from Brooklyn Arts Press.

areyououtsidethelines.wordpress.com

TO MY FATHER'S BLUE TUXEDO

The winter I turn 17 I find you hiding
in the back of his closet, wilting
on your hanger. Rumpled, crinkled,

dusted with age's mothwing-fuzz.
Baby, your blue is powdery soft,
baby-blue trim and, lapels, ruffled.

You slump, hang limp like a faggot
has just fled you, like he will his prom,
eager for a jerk-off to a tableau of tuxed jocks.

You won't recall, but I saw you once before
in a photo, posing on the body of a man
who looked like me, his hair so wet with sweat

bits of rice stuck in it. His face flush
with June sun, cheap champagne—
with simple abundance and simple poverty.

In that picture there was no fag, no boy
seeping in fear, no quarterback slamming
meaty fist into reddened palm, sick with threat.

Outside ice hangs on trees, limbs snapping:
the sound of jealousy, of a ball smacking
open palms in the end zone.

Winter will never marry us.
It is a haven too cold for love—or even fear.
Stay with me: the closet is a warm place to hide.

MY PAPA'S FAULT

Each sprint would steal my breath;
to 'go long' made me dizzy.
A gut of rocks felt like death,
and my pass was way too prissy.

'Just throw it like a man.'
he said. His son, a sylph
tripping when he ran.
How could I erase myself,

just straighten my wrists?
Make the pass, or slam my knuckles
against the locker if I missed?
And still my knees would buckle

when he lowered his head,
to hide the hurt in his eyes—
the guilt it wasn't him instead
and the wish it were *him* I despised.

PLUM

    The waves crashing woke you, and you untangled our bodies.
Your limbs taut and sundark and mine feeble and china-white
        had somehow grown together in the night like the dune's pillow weeds.

    Your shock at being here, the golden feathers of your bangs
brushing against my lips, was a cough, a whispered 'What the fuck'.

    I wish I had laughed

    when your canoe-shaped feet caught in the sandy, wrinkled sheets
and you swore again, nearly toppled (so clumsy!) as you slipped on

    the still-damp swimsuit, the sound like a zipper zipped down.
So this was how it began, how it ended: you scribbling a note—'Gone
        to Mickey D's for a coffee, some grub', stopping for a moment

    (I held my breath)

    to stare at a gray seagull, cawing out to some small thing
drowning in the Atlantic shoals. And as you locked the door and left,
    I held in a single sob, a whole plum caught in my throat,

    and watched the sky turn shades of plum
to goddamn shades of plum.

SENSORIUM
The First Five Years

1

The sickly sweet smell
of bread-still-baking
wafting from the end
of the bed, a yeast
your feet put off.

2

The tremble of your voice,
singing over and over the same
measure of a madrigal of kissings,
(the song that won you States
in high school, the scare-
crow with golden pipes)...

I feel the notes slide
into the past, slough off
you and stick to me
as I prune in the bath—
hoping that if I remain still,
no ripples, no breath,
you'll move on, finally
lose the harmony.

3

The peel of skin
from your blooming pec
as a tattoo of the phoenix
burns deep in gold, purple...
before disappearing
under my tiny hands
in milky swirls of
cool, cool oatmeal lotion.

4

The taste of your breath
—after too much wine—
and your skin, still asleep,
steeping in the humid fog
of a summer drowse...

the imagined taste of honey
as a bumblebee lands on the red
rim of the empty wine glass
set daringly on the nightstand's edge.

5

The fine blond hair
I curl into my fingers,
the damp feeling
of your wet face
against my shoulder
after you tell me about him,
and plead for me to stay.

BLOOD IN THE CUM

1

When he makes love,
he imagines himself
wrapping delicate packets
of precious white tea
in crisp squares of pink tissue.

2

He hides, under the swirling
chest hairs I kiss, what he says
are spider bites from our lovemaking.
The hives spread and mottle,
like a web of broken capillaries.

3

A poet, he cheats at the game
of diagnosis: a love poem
is his way—to kiss—to sew
our two mouths shut,
with thread so thin it's invisible.

4

He says, *The blood in the cum,*
is the scarlet ribbon
in an egg's albumen,
a mistake of embryonic petals
curling in its center.

FINDING AN EGG IN THE WATER

Plucked
from the snow
you are moon
cold.

The shell of you
is rough with bumps
like taste buds.

Under your surface
a crack
is whining
its way
to a hairline.

I tuck you
in the warm
pocket
of my thick
wool coat

Please...
stay put
as I foot
about the city
looking for—
oh, who
knows! —
a first love
or proof
of alien life.

Until then,
please
do not break.
I would lose
what little
I've left.

LUSTER

With nothing left, he pauses
on a stoop on Marlborough, poses

shirtless for passersby. He clips
off all his thick chestnut hair—

strands catch the wind, drift
drowsily through the air.

A man without past or present
stops to watch the descent.

A brick-red heat wavers
as they reach a mutual gaze:

their bodies absorb the blush
of a summer light that turns

naked skin into luster,
today into tomorrow.

KANGAS JAMES

conqueror boy's grin

James Kangas is a semi-retired academic librarian. He lives in Flint, Michigan, and plays the viola in a regional orchestra. His poems have appeared in many magazines including *Atlanta Review*, *Connecticut Review*, *The New York Quarterly*, *Tampa Review*, and *West Branch*. The following pieces, some in slightly different versions, were originally published in these magazines:

Bay Windows: "Mr. America"

Chiron Review: "Dazzleblitz Tutorial," "Mining Town"

Gerbil: "Two Musketeers"

The James White Review: "Agnus Dei"

The Panhandler: "The Museum of Natural History"

RFD: "Butch Guys: An Aesthetics," "The Cashier in the Sporting Goods Store," "Sphincter Ani"

The Windless Orchard: "Breath of Eden"

"Breath of Eden" also appeared in *Between the Cracks: The Daedalus Anthology of Kinky Verse*, G. Dillard, ed. (Daedalus Pub. Co, 1996).

MR. AMERICA

The young body builder in the laundromat
gazes back, his blaring baby
in a wicker basket, his hands busy folding
towels, happy loops that have dried
his black hair, every twist. We have met
like this before, but for the first time

this Monday evening, as I lay down
The Norman Conquest, untangle my spun
rainbow from the 50 cent washer, he drifts
over and asks nonchalantly what I study
(as if he couldn't read), in his arms
his child: banner, trumpet, shield.

THE CASHIER IN THE SPORTING GOODS STORE

Baiting me with one glance, enough
to bury the hook, you have no
intentions but to sneer me to the dirt
to gasp and thrash around, the angler
angled. Still, I can't not sigh,
can't not stare. Are you deeper
than a sardine tin, I wonder?

The fit of your skin obsesses me
like the beauty that yanked once, whipped
the pole double, and shone in the water,
lithe, iridescent, never to come home
succulent to my table with butter
and capers (that fabled Thanksgiving), never
to yield to my lips one sweet nibble.

THE MUSEUM OF NATURAL HISTORY

Scrubbing Saturdays all spring
at the junior high carwash
bought an 8th grade Chicago, one
day on the town, two in the bus.
In the Y lobby, the peerless
paired up till the class tough
and I were assigned a room

on the nineteenth floor. Who
could sleep so high—the leprous
pigeons on the fire escape?
Who could talk to him? Try
as I might, he didn't grunt
one reply, didn't glance at me.
But then, heaven had never

answered me either, all those pleas
to be one of the guys.
Half our afternoon in the Field
Museum, I stood in front of
the naked mummies, one caved-in
child, their skin like parchment
shrink-wrapped to their bones.

What a way to end up—forsaken
by Osiris, stripped, on display.
All night in the room, I thought of
nothing but their lurid fate. That
and Jack Tucker's solid body
on the next bed, the ultimate
dumb god to pray to for favors.

DAZZLEBLITZ TUTORIAL

It wasn't in a lecture hall one learned
the art that made all the other pale.
It wasn't in a studio gaping at
a canvas of electric blue larkspurs
in vast north or skylight light. It was
night in the student union where
our eyes had met for weeks, and now
he asked me if by chance I had the time
to have coffee with him, and the stars
out the Gothic windows winked *yes,*
oh, he's as cute as a puppy, he will
make you happy, and the gold-blond
oak wainscoting exhaled a whiff of
tung oil as if to approve.
                            In his
rented room in a rambling Victorian
we had some perfumed herb tea, I think,
cup after cup, and then our clothes
started to come undone and his kisses
were each a torch and then his tongue
was all over me, reaching (could it be?)
into every orifice and I went wild with
ecstasy, wild with (as far as I knew)
love, and then he flashed his suave
conqueror boy's grin and I saw that
I would want always to study the flesh
in full lather—how the nerves... jerk,
how the body can withstand such voltage.

TWO MUSKETEERS

Sprawled in your jalopy,
banner friends since diapers,
we laughed at our history of
apple cooning, camping shacks,
shooting rats at the town dump.
Stars were like baseballs
studding the sky, two or three
streaking on past the outfield
towards cosmic ash. You'd
gone to hell (at least
purgatory) in Vietnam, had
a beeline life sketched out
ahead of you. I'd been
in college and was going
in circles the way a dog
sniffs a throw rug
for a place to lie down.
Was I asking for acceptance?
Is that why I told you how
my heart sometimes had fits
but not around girls?
Ten beats of silence.
If it were deer season
I'd shoot you, you said,
as though I'd spat on your
sister, as though knowing me
would somehow transform you
to trash.

AGNUS DEI

The works of God
outshine the works of man, my friend
Alfred would say ex cathedra (ex
Catholics even say such), and I think
you'd agree with him.
                             We could be
in Chartres staring at the incomprehensible
stone marvel begun in the 12th century,
hell-bent on touching heaven,
and you'd notice the pretty boy lounging
on the steps of the south transept.

MINING TOWN

Two prepubescent boys (well really, Jeffrey, you
had edged towards your body's flux ahead of me)—
a sort of brash, precocious knight and page,
we fought with stick swords in the woods
behind the school, contriving our own legend
in that blueprint, pastel, company town, so new
that ground had not been broken for a boneyard,
and all the houses looked the same, and families
came and went. We were brats on the streets
at Halloween: paraffined windows in our wake;
doorsteps graced with luminaries (flaming paper
bags of dog shit) as we knocked, and ran.
Down by the mud-red river, you pioneered
at being adult. I was dumbstruck when you stuck
your penis into the pulp of a ripe cantaloupe
you'd cut a hole in, going straight to the heart
of the thing as though it were heaven.
You pressed me to try it, but I had to beg off
it seemed so uninviting, and I was so clearly
the amateur. When out of the blue, my father
quit the mine, I had a month as your chum
to mull the umpteen parts I couldn't comprehend
about the mad, desirous business of the body.
And then the day before we moved, at dawn,
like an omen, you cropped up in my dreams,
a prince I was servant to (it's the image of you
I've still got filed in my brain)—fleshing out
as you were, drenched in sweat from our afternoon
run to the river, grinning as you undid your buttons.

SPHINCTER ANI

In one respect it functions
the way an eye's iris does

or a camera's shutter,
opening and closing

pupil, aperture (even scant
light permits a picture).

A floodgate, it keeps
sludge in, lets it

aptly go
when it works well.

It can be viewed
as foul, unspeakable.

It can be viewed as
something to keep

one's hams tidy,
a social necessity.

It is simply an odd
muscle one can look at,

dear Horatio, in more
ways than there are

flower species in India.
What backwater is it hasn't

heard there are legions
who think of their own

as portals to pleasure
grottoes, places not unlike

mouths that love
to get filled with food?

BUTCH GUYS: AN AESTHETICS

It is a walk (sometimes
known as hunk swagger)
that declares *Tiger
in these pants wants
out and wants it now
and wouldn't you like to
fondle him.* Or it's how
the guy shows no need
of you, that cock of his
Greek god head that says
*Fuck this world, it can't
touch me.* It's the man
on the big screen with
the damnedest grin, or
the sullen one (two!—
it's hardly fair—four-star
jocks), take your pick,
they know they've got
what you crave, just eat
your hot-rocks heart out.
And it's Boy Brawn down
the street slaving over
his car, into the very
guts of it, grease up to
his elbows, in his yellow
hair, young Siegfried
of the East Side, who
doesn't know you itch
seeing him bare, belt up,
doesn't know you look.
The gestures, the postures
are learned behavior
(these magicians have
largely become their art),
and though it's nine-tenths
artifice, it fascinates so
who wouldn't stare for hours
if given a choice spot
to glut eyes on heaven,
although some mealy-mouthed
or dandied-up, tight-assed

types might claim no whit
of interest in it all,
admit nothing. Zip.

BREATH OF EDEN

After one adolescent toot
when you came over to sleep it off
in my adolescent bed, my friend,
virgins the two of us, surely, drawn
towards naked worlds we would soon plunge into,

I woke early (if I slept at all)
wanting to touch you, but instead
slipped from the sheets' cocoon to the chair
where your T-shirt and jeans lay strewn, knelt
to bury my face in them and breathe

you in as I'd breathe in the odor
and pollen from a rose deep
into my lungs and blood. Nothing
since then has intoxicated me
like the perfume of that flesh-scented garden.

MILES
FRANK J

bourgeois-homonormative

Frank J Miles, who holds a B.A. from Rutgers College and an M.A. from Columbia University, is a writer whose work has appeared in *CRUSHfanzine*, *Mary: A Literary Quarterly*, *This Is FYF*, *Philadelphia City Paper*, and *The Huffington Post*. In his spare time, he volunteers with several New York City youth-advocacy organizations dedicated to making an impact for the rising number of homeless American LGBT youth, regardless of race, class, gender, or geography, as well as the devastating number of U.S. teens who have contracted HIV/AIDS. Presently, he is turning his blog about cultural-war melodrama into a magazine called *Junkpunch*. He also is embarking on a nationwide "Eat Pray Love" to San Francisco, Austin, Portland, Santa Fe, and Albuquerque and will settle down in whichever city is his best fit.

deweylightfoot.wordpress.com

TRADE POEM 1

My Fag Stag harpies:
"Until you leave the Tames for the Trade, duder.
It's not about
not findin' a pleasant
good
or not findin' someone charmin', mang.
It's about the low
maintenance and the Stuff of someone, boyo. Guy
on the ball,
homie—not just guy
peekabooin' his echo and mirror—
is a simple, kind
delight to be around, bruddah."

Zhooshed to the 9s like Marcia Brady,
Tames
at organic bodega, on elliptical, in steam room,
at happy hour at bar, Grindr, scene,
farmers' market, gallery, afterparty, Splash
afterparty, Jeff Lewis afterparty, Reichen Lehmkuhl afterparty,
tanning bed, manscaping den, salon for petite dogs,
"Sex and the City 2" midnight
show before opening day in Kips Bay,
depth of afterbirth and cornmeal, psyche of Chrissy
Snow.

Hyena breakups in the raw,
bourgeois-homonormative,
incarnadine vein of: "I'm out." Meltdown!
"You're meh! I told you to get to steppin'. I'm done." Shrill!
"And out. O-U-T." Melodrama!
"Done and done." Hysteria!
"It feels like seventh grade." Man down!
"And worse than I'm not
into you is: I'm going to say I'm not
into you somewhat kind of,
but act like I'm
into you somewhat kind of." Dishonesty! Cowardpunk!
"Kick, curb, next!" Ferocity of the Gods!
"Next. Check!" Asystole!

A dreary ache tenders
toward vigor woe & oomph whoredom,
a lost generation,
another, of tugging soldiers shell-
shocked in vain
in the passion trenches.

Rinse, wash, do over again—
oooh,
look, it's shiny, a surface of huh prancing like Peter Pan, a lad
who lifts, a flibbertigibbet in brawn,
and
that's it.
In Manhattan, like modern art,
you catch only the urgency of now
before he starts fetching around,
like puce, the shade
of fleas,
for the next.
You're dustbin of ancient history
in favor of the followed by,
the afterward whoa and the wave.
He's ever searching and always probing
for the first,
the first
that stops time, beyond measure,
the first
levitating remembrance
of ascension blast and pinnacle daylight past, *ab aeterno*,
the earliest pop from time immemorial, *à bout de soufflé*,
breathless like Eden.
Until you leave the Tames for the Trade…

TRADE POEM 2

"Until you leave the Tames for the Trade,"
my Fag Stag molests,
"You need a new
type,
duder.
You need to go
a little more
borin', mang.
Not lackluster,
but
less flash
and
more Matter, boyo.
Like a coupe,
a Civic,
broad shoulders, sturdythick, bushy,
like a 'Dude, whatever'
Brody—
periods not exclamation
points, eye-catching, chill—
no chaser,
raspy
voice like swallowed gravel, sweet man
of
heft—
there's
there
there,
homie,
as bristle-velvet
and secure as the Green
underneath.
Look for gentle
eyes, bruddah—it works.
Until you leave the Tames for the Trade…
No gamechanger, you
just keep playin'
D-III ball."

Until you leave the Tames for the Trade.

WTF's Trade?!

In 2011?!

A dreamy gayboy
fantasy,
doctrine of the vacuous, fetish of the masculine,
we unthinkingly
overidealize? And are supposed to?
Or risk
excommunication and censure and leper isolation?
Some grunt-machismo, heteronormative,
punch-me-in-the-face-and-tell-me-to-shut-up
archetype we chain
ourselves to the oven for or gamble
bruises out and in?

Trade, what are you? Who are you? Are you…

Maybe he's…

Boom-boom chichi
drink with South American cactus
and some Uzbekistani flavor?
No, beer,
American,
or from an easily familiar country where hops
aren't for lawn animals.
Follows up, follows through.
Santa Claus traits, exercise regimen. With embonpoint muscles.
Cheese on the bread, buttered
on its slab, croaky-voiced,
spells arugula
like
lettuce,
thinks pied-à-terre's
a glistening keep-fit
dancers
in Benvolio tights do.

Doesn't know it:
Manliness on legs, built for immovability and stevedoring,
carpenter arms trading pliers with electricity wires for Con Ed,
never rebuffing a toothy, beatific smile,
like a violin sweep to harmony, as gloriously radiant
as a 5-pound-bonylean, "Footloose" swish to a tribal house drum beat.

Good egg.

Texture rugged,
transformative—
fully mature and well-rounded like a salt-miner bear
with a hardware store downtown he built with buttressing bricks
and naked hands that can change a tire kaput and bake a mean casserole
from basic things found lodged in tin cans and unresealable plastics,
while his prideful mouth gleamingly idioms and slangs
the recipe
from juvie memory
aloud in a cocoa-butter drawl because he only does
path of least resistance, action not talk, rowing to shore.

All angles sharp
and lips full,
ginger, and thick blond hands.
Castle no pale. Danger
and twinkle,
beach no waves, warm
and there, beneath and present. Here…

TRADE POEM 3

Here,
on our fourth date,
once I became dog-tired,
my get-
up-
and-go whacked and my heart
meek,
with a brain frothy and so-so and memory full
of serrate tears and vain corridors,
prole eyes,
a pant withdrawn,
philistine fingers,
sleeves stitched of awkward and coy,
I was Byronic hero trapped
in middlebrow Rohmer
played by Henry James,
combing
through dry ass and blue balls
and witty
one-liners,
building pathos,
evacuating emotional depth.

"Get out your head,
open
wide to my gasping, gasping spark.
Shut up.
You should be in me by now.
Please,
Trade,
please,
Soma me, with ember and whirl,
into a higher beg for humanity.
I've been waiting,"
echo
my shell-shocked thought and scar tissue, "for you—
rough and tumble,
butch and delicious, heteronormative down to the socks,
luminous face,
freight-elevator hand, right and left and right,
voice of transcendence,

guava tongue,
Saint Ignatius of Loyola pendant
on a stretched fire-red chain,
David biceps and Guevara pec tat
quietly marooned beneath your navy shirt 9-to-5—
for 3,285 hours."

Come on!

Only connect!

Cock and hole.

Handsome like Tenōchtitlān keeps chatting
about green maps,
blah,
conquistador adventures for treasure and booty, concord and silence,
yadda,
meepmeep shoals and cerulean-battered rocks, and beachy things.
I, jaded and stiff,
want to mute him
with an eloquently amaranth kiss. Buzz, pow, dash, hush, sigh, bang.

For starts.

I want to murmur across the undersized table:
"As 1 of our happy little congress of 2,
I'm going to paw you: Oh, so benevolently."
If benevolence were bloodshed. I act,
with nothing,
drooping,
nerves decrescendo into humility and elegy.

NORRIS ERIC

lord of lightning

Eric Norris was born in Buffalo in 1968. These days he works as a law librarian in New York City. He enjoys swimming, running, and reading Soseki Natsume in his spare time. Though not always in that order and not always in Japanese. His work has appeared in *Q-Review*, *The Barefoot Muse, Ganymede Unfinished, Ganymede, Bay Windows*, and the poetry anthology, *This New Breed: Gents, Barbarians and Bad Boys 2*.

PREFACE TO A LIFE

'Fair seed time had my soul. Then I grew up.'
—William Wordsworth, *The Prelude*, Book I

A LIFE
Part I.

I have a dirty secret to disclose
Before we start here. Can I be candid?
This isn't the profession that I chose.
I'm no poet. I don't understand it.
Like any child, I dreamed of writing prose:
My box of cereal, The Daily Planet,
Proust—they spoke to me. And poetry—
It seems a rotten way to treat a tree.

Your poet only has three subjects: love,
Despair and death. Maybe the odd flower.
My numbers here are estimates. And rough.
I have just drawn zero for an hour
Which seemed like an eternity—enough
Time to admit the limits of my power:
The Muses call me, but I cannot sing.
Sure, I can give you Shakespeare, gargling,

That's simple: he is in this huge bathroom,
A Dixie cup in hand, an inch of Scope
Bubbling in his throat. Scope, I presume,
Not Listerine, which kills bacteria, hope,
You, and me, and everything—ka-boom!
William was hygienic—not a dope.
I once was his—let's just call me a guest—
Since I was underage and such a pest.

My own facilities are less extensive:
I've got the standard toilet, white, a small
Bathtub, a sink. Talcum powder gives
My place a pale, imperial air. Each fall
That fragile autumn light, for which I live,
Will form a golden window on the wall
Right above those faucets—there. I'm sorry
Faucets don't figure larger in my story,

But try to let your mind fill in these gaps.
Use whatever odds and ends you wish:
Your own experiences, marbles, maps,
A plum stone glistening in a glass dish,

Your favorite pair of underwear—those chaps—
Leftovers from the rodeo in Bliss.
A big bermuda onion. I don't know.
Something should suggest itself. Let go.

Daydreaming is a thing I like to do
When I have these imaginary needs.
Most authors have a strategy or two.
John Milton summoned scrolls, papyrus reeds,
Imported at great expense from the past. It's true,
Lord Byron also dabbled in some deeds
Of great antiquity—at least on paper.
My own involvement in that curious caper

Consisted of a week in Italy,
Spent cruising, boozing, having the want ads
Read to me over oranges and coffee.
"Now, here's one," Byron said, "Do you drive cabs?
Have abs? Do you crave immortality?
I'm looking for an epic hero, lads:
If you are muscular, can swim, or fly,
Reply by photograph—and don't be shy!"

His Lordship cut the ad out with a smile
I do not have the skills to recreate.
I had been out of work for a long while,
And since great beauty seems to be my fate,
I did not add this clipping to the pile
Of orange peels I placed beside my plate.
I glanced down at my boxers on the floor.
I always knew I'd be a hero, or

A star, somebody special. Back in school
I did some modeling for extra money.
The teacher had me stand on a barstool
And said, "Pretend you are Apollo." He—
I have to say I felt like quite a fool,
Apollo's nowhere near as hot as me.
But they were paying people cash—ten dollars
An hour. I pretended. Students, scholars,

Each sat stiffly at his flimsy easel
While teacher twinkled, orbiting the class.
Boys glared at me, like I embodied Evil,
As if I were one huge, malignant mass
Of muscle. All except this one guy—Steve—I'll
Call him. His mouth just opened wider as
I began, quite slowly, to undress…
Excuse this small diversion. I digress.

A LIFE
Part II.

I have a feeling gaping mouths are not
The most propitious places to begin
A work of art—but I am in a spot—
A god—Apollo. Can't I be forgiven?
You work with the materials you've got.
And when you have a bunch of gifts from Heaven—
Nice teeth like these, luxurious, long hair
That bounces beautifully—you want to share.

Although I'd never send a guy to Hell
For praising his own features in this way,
Not everyone up here's so wonderful—
So I'd be careful with that resume.
Among my peers on Mount Olympus—well—
The sad divinities who now hold sway—
A somewhat jealous spirit still prevails.
Venus will extract your fingernails

If you annoy her. All I do is rhyme—
Brain a lazy reader with my lyre.
I used to pass out plagues for a good time.
I lent my son the Chariot of Fire,
He incinerated Persia. I'm
Sorry for that. Kids. Our laws require
Celestial beings to be licensed now,
For all light vehicles—from crane to cow.

Our modes of transport differ. Even here,
In Heaven, we find harmony elusive.
Although each god has been assigned a sphere
Of influence, gods can be reclusive—
Some would prefer we didn't interfere
In man's affairs. Some turn red, abusive,
Chanting, "Blah, blah, blah—not anymore—
Just look what happened with the Trojan War!"

Let Homer dwell upon that dismal plain
Where Troy once stood—that heap of stones and ash—
Her towers toppled, all those horses slain.
Life goes on, my friends. It always has.

Who needs Achilles being such a pain
In Agamemnon's ass? Give me Aeneas—
Virgil—an aqueduct in every home!
Let's follow Aeneas from Troy to Rome.

Wife near death, dad hoisted on his back,
His son, Ascanius, clutching his hand,
'Mid smoke and flames—and that spine splintering crack—
I watched Aeneas assembling his band
Of refugees—still reeling from attack—
Astonished, terrified, and angry—and
I was amazed: away these people stole,
With only life—existence—as a goal.

Now, there's a man I could work wonders with.
When the moment for departures came,
I joined the Trojan forces. I exist
Now thanks to them: Apollo. Same name, same
Athletic youth I always was—no myth:
Some gods are good at the survival game.
Since Rome was destined to devour Greece,
I felt that Heaven ought to get a piece.

I chose Olympus, naturally, and we
Crowned Jove with victory. And Zeus, poor dear,
Our late, lamented chief has been—you'll see.
It can be odd to be a god. One year
You're Lord of Lightning—next you're history—
A bunny nobody would ever fear,
Banging a drum for better batteries.
As you can tell, I am not one of these.

I am the god of prophecy. That's why
I tend to show up on the winning side—
Even when the contest is a tie.
You can't prevent the turning of the tide—
Although you are at liberty to try.
The last time that I saw the moon defied,
I heard my sister sigh, and with a shrug,
She crushed this kid's sandcastle like a bug.

Diana's rather moody for a rock,
A maiden prone to madness. Take the rage

She showed Actaeon—that bewildered buck
Who stumbled on a sliver of her image
Floating in a pool. It always struck
Me as severe—given his young age.
She sent a pack of hounds to chat with him:
They ripped the lad apart—limb from limb.

The birds still speak of him, so do the trees,
"O, Actaeon! Transformed from man to deer,
And then—a frightened fragrance on the breeze."
You may have sympathy—but let's be clear:
My sister does exactly what she please—
She's not—what is the phrase—not in your sphere.
We all have boundaries that we must obey.
Perhaps one day we won't. It's hard to say.

But when we don't, I'll tell you. At Delphi,
Cumae—wherever strange events occur—
I'll dress up as a lady, for a fee,
And murmur things to kings about your future—
Things inconsequential, friends, to me—
Since Mars, remember, is our god of war.
I'm archery, arts, medicine, the sun.
I am in charge of germs. And hydrogen.

Making music is my main concern;
The fate of you, your pets, your family,
The gases Pompeians give off when they burn,
Their density, volume, toxicity,
How many cinders children can inurn,
Are governed by a different agency.
A different deity—I should say,
Since we are all Olympians today,

Aren't we? I do not count that child—
That Cupid—mixing milk in with his wine.
"Pray, Bacchus, see his empty skull is filled
With burgundy—with visions so divine
He thinks he's God Almighty." Love has killed
More than one mortal trying to combine
The forces which set God and man apart.
Our differences aren't subtle. Life and art,

Container and contained, the wine, the skin—
The leopard, dancing, tearing off your head,
Your legs, an arm, whatever is virgin,
Or available. Somewhere I have read
Men taste more like pork than roast chicken.
Not that it really matters. I'm in bed
Most evenings well before ten o'clock—
Long before the clubs begin to rock.

Whenever gods go drinking homicide's
The general result. We drink too much.
Our lust for power is too hard to hide
From Jove—The Thunderer. I still will blush
When I remember how I almost died
One morning. Suddenly, no warning—whoosh!
I happened to be hunting for my sister:
How narrowly that arrow missed her!

T'was then, I think, I entered medicine.
"First, do no harm," I say, with emphasis.
You can thank me for aspirin, Ambien,
Peroxide, dentures, and Q-Tips. And this:
This box of Trojans—in gold foil—just in
Case anyone should try to force a kiss.
Humanity will do that. Sometimes,
Men are deaf to reason. Even rhymes.

You are exceptional. Don't get me wrong—
I love humanity. I love the lark.
I add a pinch of brilliance to his song
Each dawn—when half the planet's in the dark—
When Vulcan's snoring in his forge among
Computer guts and cannons—it's a perk.
We'll share a Milky Way on Sunday nights,
Admiring you and all your satellites.

I had Vulcan make the crystal ball
I gave Cassandra—Cassie. Pretty girl.
She hated my prophetic gift. She'd call
It cursed—called me despicable. She'd hurl
That innocent glass globe against a wall:
The silly thing thought she could change the world
By shattering it! Imagine her despair
When it bounced back and hit her. How unfair!

A LIFE
Part III.

I wonder if I'm cruel enough to be
Convincing as Apollo? I don't know.
I was born in Buffalo, you see,
The Town of Tonawanda—land of snow—
A rusty suburb of reality.
We manufactured autos, long ago.
Nothing much goes on here anymore.
Luckily, our taverns close at four.

Here, Mendelssohn wed Edwin to Kathleen
Around the time of my conception in
A battered Skylark. Dad was a Marine,
Lance Corporal. Loyal, like most Marlboro men,
They say he shot a cigarette machine
On Okinawa, from frustration, when
A pack of twenty Camels tumbled out.
Yet, I never saw him smoke. Or shout.

Mom insisted that he switch to snuff
When I arrived. They slowly separated, and
I only knew my father long enough
To miss him really—hold his massive hand
As we departed. He was soft, but tough.
Some kids need discipline, you understand.
Mom did her best. She did not spare the rod—
Her special spatula—the Wrath of God.

That spatula and I, we still survive.
We pass strange things along in my family.
Ghost stories, mostly. Like who dropped the knife
(This bayonet—my father's legacy)
Down the laundry chute. It's my belief—
And here my mother and I disagree—
The thing was cruddy. And so down it slid.
It needed washing. That's what mothers did.

I brushed my teeth and I was sent to bed
Early that night. That sort of shocked me, too.
I'm sure that in my future you saw red—
A bloody end, involving scarlet dew-

Drops, total melodrama. No. Mom said,
"Do you know how I got this big boo-boo?"
I nodded very meekly—in this style—
And pointed sadly at my brother, Kyle.

"Man hands on misery to man," of course,
Nothing could be easier than THAT.
Happiness is harder, and a source
Of great perplexity to poets—at
Least those creeps who scatter metaphors,
Like tears, across each page, without éclat,
Éclairs, or anything more pleasant. I
Sincerely hope I am not such a guy.

My mother heaved the huge, eye-rolling sigh
She usually saved for The Three Stooges.
Despite my innocence, and cuteness, I
Was tucked in tightly. Kyle burped brown juices
On his bib, not quite comprehending why.
To this day, that wicked child refuses
To admit anything—though he can talk.
And walk. He's even lost his taste for chalk.

Well, before I fix him, it is clear
We need to straighten out this dialogue.
Now, what were we discussing? Proust? Shakespeare—
He once permitted me to walk his dog
When I came over. It was pretty weird:
My mind filled up with music, then a fog,
This mist precipitated in my eyes—
I thought it was just raining. Big surprise:

I was back in the old neighborhood;
And Heaven only knows how I got there.
We moved a lot. But I was pretty good
At climbing out of trouble. My highchair
Proved to be a problem though. I could
Not master gravity. Perhaps the air
Malfunctioned. Or my wings. At least I tried.
I cracked my cranium, and cried, and cried.

God, curiosity must be the bane
Of my existence. Take this incident:

A bawling baby with a bit of brain
Exposed. Was this a portent, or the dent
Death left inside my consciousness? For pain,
I received kisses, not the monument
I wanted, carved in marble: TRAGEDY.
I need to work more on my savagery.

LUCZAK RAYMOND

a swing of unarticulated desire

Raymond Luczak is the author and editor of twelve books. His three collections of poetry include *St. Michael's Fall* (Deaf Life Press, 1996), *This Way to the Acorns* (The Tactile Mind Press, 2002), and *Mute* (A Midsummer Night's Press, 2010). He has won an Artist Recognition Grant for his poetry from Jerome Foundation and the VSA Arts of Minnesota. His novel *Men With Their Hands* (Queer Mojo, 2009) won a first-place grant for Full-Length Fiction 2003 from the Arch and Bruce Brown Foundation and first place in the Project QueerLit 2006 Contest. Nineteen of his stage plays have been performed in three countries so far. Two of his full-length documentaries have been released on DVD. Luczak's work is taught in ASL interpreter training programs as well as disability and Deaf Studies programs around the country. His forthcoming collection of poetry, *Road Work Ahead*, will be published in March by Sibling Rivalry Press.

www.raymondluczak.com

THE MOP-HAIRED BOY

Summer is a mop-haired toothy-grinned boy
who's never had to work a single day in his life.
Lanky yet never gawky, he ambles by
all the girls with petals in their hair
oozing gasps of nectar in his wake.

Full of weed-induced giggles, he lazes about
and says, "Man, what's happening," a lot.
Nights of fireflies puncture the haze of his vision.
He inhales the poppy scents of romance,
but it's not enough. So heroin it is.

He doesn't understand why nobody wants him now.
He's forgotten how one can stink after not bathing so long.
Forced to enter a methadone clinic, he cuts his hair.
Seeing his own pock-marked face in the mirror
for the first time is a terrible autumn.

WHITE PINES

    1.

A long time ago young men wishing to be tall
scaled the mast of my octopus arms
and scanned the horizon of Lake Superior
for a glimmer of Canada. Usually we were cut down.

    2.

The long prickly fur that cover my arms
shields the damp ground from the sun.
My deepened feet wade lazily in the tidal soil.
Worms sniggling around my toes itch right.

    3.

The world of men down there has its own rules.
They don't realize how us pines must band together,
weaving arms out of loneliness against the skies.
We are bred to do without women, yet we ache.

    4.

Squirrels, birds, and deer know I fathered
these woods cascading like ocean waves
up and down the Porcupine Mountains.
They know safety is complete in my shadow.

    5.

Men are always angry at how I could dominate.
My one stem is always thick and erect,
always dribbling with resin even in cold rains.
Years only strengthen my veins unlike theirs.

6.

Us pines don't say much. Just listening
to each other breathe is almost too close to sex.
I've never had a woman, but each cone dropped
is a tear for the one I never had. May each breed.

7.

Every generation us pines will catch fire.
Stripped to the color of ash, we stand barren.
In the powdery soil are some of our buried cones,
laced with seeds that will split and remember.

8.

Divide me among an ocean of short men
made tall with the affliction of seafaring.
My absence will enable all my children
the first kiss of sun, the first drench of rain.

SIX GALLERY, SAN FRANCISCO: OCTOBER 7, 1955
The first time Allen Ginsberg reads "Howl" in public

Fog from down the bay unfurled its mystic kisses from deep inside America yet to be plumbed and renamed, only to find itself pressed against the glass windows, already fragile from the constant bombing of words and lines by the six poets swearing to take on the world of academic and elitist poetry. Claps flitted around the tiny gallery after each poem uttered, no longer a dream but a reality anchoring and climbing inside the listener's ear. Then came the fifth poet, all shaven and bespectacled not yet full of Jack Kerouac's "first thought, best thought" writing philosophy that would later render him downright impotent some three decades later, but there he was, drunk from cheap wine with a sheaf of typewritten papers, check-marked with constant corrections and deletions and reinsertions. As he lumbered through his poem for Carl Solomon, the train-clanging lines that once seemed like whispers in his own dreams began to eject powerful gusts of steam, he couldn't stop, he was finally waking up, the words were smooth as glass down the rail of mountains bye-bye now, the parchy hunger for wetness inside his mouth didn't matter, each word became a ghost floating off the sheet of paper, all became a crowd intermingling among the sharp gasps of shock from those watching this man losing himself in the love he'd felt for Carl and the hurt for America, America, America. The glass windows so tightly screwed on were pushed to the corners, ready to shatter from the hot air of ghosts and gasps mixing into a nitrous gas. The words so carefully spewed out of that young man's mouth began to surge and rise up a flood of emotion where all there drowned in while William Blake and Walt Whitman, now eternal comrades, bobbed in their glass-bottomed dinghy, and looked blankly down at the very strange pipsqueak with his horn-rimmed glasses who had absolutely no idea what a Pandora's tub he was about to unplug.

INEVITABILITY, 2005
In memory of our basset hound
Elsa 1994 - 2007

One morning I will depart and leave her
behind with the man I once loved.
On the perch of her sofa near the door,
she will wait days and weeks as before,
sighing with her sleepy eyes fixed
on that door sure to click open suddenly
with my voice calling her once again.

How does anyone explain to a dog
the awful distance one must travel
not for just a few months but years
when all she knows are feet, treats,
and urine markings left behind by dogs
she's sniffed once or twice before?
Around the block is her domain.

One night I will return and meet her
wagging furiously in spite of her years,
her thick tender bones not as limber
with her fat pads that once slapped at
my hands when she lolled on her back.
Though her thinned face will have whitened,
she will insist on sniffing me, disbelieving.

I gaze into her chocolate-melted eyes,
warmed by the amber fire of familiarity.
Does she understand how I yearn for her
to be free of confusion when I finally go?
Will I ever be strong enough to look her
in the eye and lie that I've never left her?
I can't, can't put my heart to sleep like this.

NEAR NORRIE PARK

Montreal River smoothed
its brown ripples, sprung
free of wrinkles, over the cement
dam. Everything was a giggle.
There was never a stain of desire.

Straddling my bike at fifteen, I stared
for hours, wondering how people could
hide their aches to touch each other,
and how a wall could restrain
slinky spurts with such grace.

FLUSHES

1.

The teal tiles lined the walls,
a damp prison air,
as I sat on a bench,
its paper stretched taut
from end to end,
awaiting the executioner
to come a-calling
with his squirtgun,
filled with warm water.
I turned off my hearing aids
and took out my earmolds.
He tilted my head,
flushed the fluid deep
into my ear canal,
which induced shivers
of nightmare,
and tilted me again
to let remnants of ear wax
tickle me on its way out.

2.

Swirling around in the stainless steel bowl
just underneath my dripping earlobe
were words of my classmates
("Runt of the class." "Crybaby." "Stupid!")
remade into tiny turds floating.

Disgust filled my tongue but I forced down
the rising puke of loneliness.

It was only temporary. I would one day
restore my hearing. I would finally catch
all their jokes and inherit their bravado.
I would be one of them.

3.

Leaving the doctor's office,
I looked down Aurora Street.
The world seemed a different tint.
People didn't take notice.

My ears were reborn.
I never wore my earmolds
for at least an hour.
I liked the way the wind tumbled
into my ear canals
as they dried. The wind was
all I could feel. I was happy.

As soon as I heard these jeering boys,
I wanted the wax back in my ears again.

IN THE GUNS SECTION

Hanging us upside down under bad lights,
the store must think we women guns are weak.
We're too petite for quarterly quotas.
The blood settles in the top of our heads,
a throbbing squishy vise on our eyeballs.
We watch the pot-bellied humans strut up,
show their IDs, and fondle the men guns
posed sideways like centerfolds below us.
They sprout faggot-bashing like poetry.
We radar for their bedraggled housewives,
their shopping carts full of babies in squall.
Our keg-powdered faces aren't loud enough.
Somebody, please pull our triggers and shoot
those fat assholes. We've got splitting migraines.

THE CUTTING
for J.O.

He was my stalk, and I his branch.
I protected him from the birds
that swooped down, hoping for an overlooked berry
hanging from my arm.

Instead I was deemed too large.
Lopped off, I sulked in a glass of water on the sill,
my roots whitened raw with tears.
The sun filtered in my water was pure morphine.

I grew gnarly nails from hunger and madness.
Finally allowed into soil, I mined
rich ores of minerals and nutrients. I swore
never to let go. My muscular roots thickened.

As I turned all my eyelids upward to the sun,
I felt a tender itch sprout off my side.
I cradled him until he was ready to go off on a limb.
One day, my boy, they'll take you away from me.

COWBOY'S LAMENT

Sheriff, please look the other way and blow
an outlaw wind my way through dem alleys
where I spend lonely nights singin', drinkin',
and whorin' with stinky lowlifes on the lam.
Time's a pig's trough of unbathed mem'ries.

I don't care what grub I chow down, long
as my belly stops reckonin'. Hell, I'd cream
for anythin' passin' for affection.
Hey, Sheriff, pour me a flask of kisses.
This town sure could use some rain.

In the sunsets before I doze off, I see
my ol' cowboy restin' on his tired horse
in the distance. Pray make my desert heart
a tumbleweed rollin' faster back to him.
I am an unsigned ransom note.

BUDDING DRAG QUEEN

Long toes stoked forward
into glossy red heels

Feet arched flawlessly
not a indentation from tight shoes

Ankles sculpted from marble
a match striking the floor with each sway

Calves groomed with lean muscle
a cup of hand shielding the sinews

Knees jointed with lightning
a swing of unarticulated desire

If only you had legs, attitude, skirt,
and a lilting sashay to match.

BURODNY JAY

impossible fathers

Jay Burodny, from Nashville, Tennessee, makes his first print appearance in this issue of *Assaracus*.

our first
JOHN STAHLE
discovery

IMPOSSIBLE FATHERS LONELY TOGETHER

You will learn how semen thinks
if you take it in and quickly drink
its sour filling, the bleached saliva,
the nightcrawler's hug, morning at night,
cuddled with the moon of its color
bound, aching, sweet on your tongue,
my tongue, ours together, can't yet
tell if mine is yours or if we're wet
from my love, this love for you,
grand if only you had a womb
that would hold me inside it
and with you my shoulders
would carry it through to you
until we formed something new.
If only you would learn my semen
doesn't like your tract, it gags,
it guesses what we are, rightly, fags,
but it is still our food as we relax
on you on me on the world of wax
which melts under us, swallows whole
our couple, this couple, this undue role
in which I gag, too, sometimes on you,
dark in here in the candle-room,
alone in the burn as the saw cuts through.
Where did you go? Curl in me?
When my left and right lungs are free
will you bury me in your chest?
Will you hold and kill and kiss me,
this dust, kiss even this dust sheet
which is me, incidentally,
pressed flat like it always has been
when people must speak so silent
and shy away and never defend
their art or love or chemical science:
but this is a promise, you there,
act like we're strangers to each other,
they won't know the difference
or fuel their will to bother,
us to bother, me dead, you fodder
for the next round-up of impossible fathers.
Love! It knows you through and through,

though I know you better, I know you too,
even deaf and nearing dumb I see our food
sprouting from what fruits from you,
I crave it, so leave it there, please leave it soon.

THEY WHO PASS AS BROTHERS

A boy strolls—in humid dark—
foremost his face turns the palest
when he gives his heart away
and the rest of him freely—
and when he forgives he weeps,
next to old men at market
who themselves never hear it from him—
and turns the bone of his back toward
the sun when the sun would ask
for a bronzer him, a human flask—
and must wash his whiskey away
in the darker sleep than a casket may
for his liver is a wilting jack—
and he learned to whistle through
broken teeth, but a few intact,
learned to bite his tongue in half—
and forgets nibbles issue muffled oft
in both the ecstatic touch
and in the dullness of an unlit croft—
and what braced him was not another one
but a bedroom, a father's son,
the question "What have ye done
with me tonight, for me alone?"—
and the dusk here accompanies him home
on his stroll from the gravestones
and the gasping mouth he sucked, once, no longer.

FATHERS AND CIGARS AND I ONLY HAVE ONE

shit love,
he tasted like tobacco and looked a mighty sight
in that cotton towel, that bit of greece 'round his hips,
the geezer was made of sandalwood and expense
   even fouler things, like the kike word,
and he worked hard didn't he when he passed
me the ball and the other under him and like a vulture
I just peered and listened for him to let me be the cannibal
   for a few moments with his flesh over my gums,
but he tasted too bad all over and he tasted like tobacco
all over and his father, his father walked in again
smoking that cigar and his boy smelled so much of the perfume
   that like a vulture I peered while the cigar met the boy

A BODY'S WORK

Must throw out the whole
new thing, be it a rice dinner
or a shirtless man bent over
the pedestal of forming iron,
too much iron, like the liver
always to purge its face
through the dim gouge of night
which wakes itself half-dead
somewhat like its people,
nude then, vomiting but awake,
curled over each as the other
but nodded off like their toes
still bent over, knowing not of tense,
half-alive and curled thence
until unwashed dawn comes along
and works, works until the work is done.

HELD A STUTTER

Learned euthermia not from
a lowly leather tome nor the weed
that fed that body-digging mud
hot enough to burn them down to bed,
learned euthermia from what I laid on instead.
Oh the supply of psychiatry
over bootstrap and stretch,
on a hook then like a hand
scooping up its arm from Pazuzu,
as I remember it, euthermia from you.
And other fools who dragged themselves
out the tar-pits what god laid on
& threw what was left for the earth,
who hums, whose humming heartbeat
feels now a concert like this one ought,
knows it once was laid on then was not.

POUR THE POOR

And so oak splinters
into its substrate faces,
those blue and those underage
who turn around and over through
their rings, held high above,
when they fall apart and sing of love.
Or do they? Is it else a grimace
for their heated breath,
else a nod of the eye at
subtle gonads that grow in light
like the wide algae or the flower.
How they grow, and sow, and sow
their nutrients far to the north,
where snowfall covers all the floor
in a floor of babbling sooth
how all end up and end up soon.
Live alone eighty years, come along
but mute and deaf of song then
tell another they're meant to mate
rather than drink or breathe a fume.
How else would a hermit look
if he were not a party of himself
talking to the rest of his split head?

THREE DAYS

As the liver dies so does it live
in muscles made tenement such
that other things path off
for ridicule makes the organ drive,
harder 'til its exhalation passes out.
Or it dies, says it thrives,
but makes a man drunker and drunker
until it makes no mention
of beauty or biscuit or dimension,
simply goes away, left three days,
have three days until a man goes away.
Until on his bed. Says a man
writhed and begged and begged and begged.

A NEEDY GOD

The haste of it when poison adulterate
grew legs, two legs upon the perch
over this gasping sea of people
who want to breathe but need to rest.
They are the late, the meridian,
a number of oiled masses all the same
in their hush, in their somatic gather.
When does a body grow itself a mind?
Or a father his fathering, where lurches
his beak into the hole in the ground
perspiring a kernel one day made human.
How do they congregate in the nervous shade
of hunger, in the intellect of weather,
who like me pardons them their wastes?
They grow, almost by intent, somehow
likened to the human regent whose foul
yearn reaches through each salting duct
into a ventricle of blood which hugs
so tightly each wall, tightly enough
to burst through yapping in the world rough.
They shuffle in the poison beneath me
in the basin all together in the strange
pulpit long enough for a private touch
but short, too short for their very much.
A human, and a human, nearly countless,
each head dust, each groin a fountain,
inclined toward my home and greedy for my gold
yet sweet, when young, slim, hunched, and old.
I will keep them, though I cannot know them,
would rather bury them than have them sold.

PEDERAST BEAT

   I did not retreat
because mum slapped it into me
from birth that if I should,
I'd become cement cartoon
and learn what a sex is
   blandly from the intimation
   of intelligence in a nutshell
   which could only become else
   livened by connections to cave and draco
   ties to cement by anima and sounds
learning what a sex is
of men and men or toys
voyeurs and tours and livid
boys upon return from uterus
that hailed wash on cemented walls
alive and pounding animated
   as if I were a boy again
   thrusting his thirst into pillow cotton
   bushes as if I were a boy again
   without this dwarf dividing my knees
fall with the power of lust
and education that learns from
devils and those men or toys
that tour the world and speak
chalance and righteousness to ignorance
transformed by events
in which they learned what a sex is
   before I did
   regret what I had learned
   they told my oldness and ancient fire
   I'd no lover or lane or
   tinder to burn, that I was
a boy learning
what a cunnus was
or a penis was dished
by lessons in French Lecons
of fidelity and men
taking their take and divisions,
   I counted One
two
   three but I couldn't count again

   97 is too old so I can count only to
three
   when I die a century, in memory
   older
than me
   the nineteen hundreds, the learned
teen
   century where bombs bridled buildings,
erections
and falsities
   learned men learnt what lurid meant
demented men
lysergic cleanly energy
vortallied until my tongue
was wet from the dry region
and I cried wetly on my
   face of a century
   counting to Three, and prosody captured
   no thing but a hellion rebellious boy
   taught his lessons; taught his
meanings.

MILLS
STEPHEN SCOTT

this could be the end

Stephen S. Mills has an MFA from Florida State University. His poems have appeared in *The Gay and Lesbian Review*, *PANK Literary Magazine*, *Velvet Mafia*, *The New York Quarterly*, *The Antioch Review*, *The Los Angeles Review*, *Knockout*, *Ganymede*, *Poetic Voices Without Borders 2* and others. His first book titled *The Hanky Code*, co-written with Bryan Borland, is due out in 2011 by Lethe Press. He is also the winner of the 2008 Gival Press Oscar Wilde Poetry Award. He currently lives in Orlando, Florida, with his partner and his dog.

joesjacket.blogspot.com

CONFESSIONS OF AN OPEN RELATIONSHIP

*"And the Lord God said, 'It is not good
that man should be alone'" –Genesis 2:18*

I. THE DECISION

It was your idea over drinks at a chain restaurant,
where the hostess, dressed in black, giggled, unable

to walk in her high-heels. Rational, business-like,
we talked of sex with other men, of adventure, daring

the other to say yes as we laughed at our growing
erections hidden beneath cloth napkins. Erections

that lasted until we reached our bed, our bodies moving
to the rhythm of four years together, each crevice

excavated long ago by younger, nervous hands.
Afterward, in the florescent light of our bathroom,

I wiped the semen from your chest, caught your face
in the mirror catching mine, and knew the decision.

II. THE RULES

"Safety always. A trusting face.
No strangers in the house.
Always a top. No giving oral."

We write them in my journal
for safekeeping. You suggest
a scrapbook of boys we fuck,

and we shake hands
like the night we met,
both nervous, standing

in the hallway of my dorm,
you reaching your hand out
to touch me for the first time.

III. ONLINE

What if Adam's rib had created another Adam?
Would the whole human race have faded away

like internet boys who parade before us offering
blowjobs, fuck buddies, glory hole encounters,

then disappear forever? Would two men have found
a way to keep us going, to breed new life?

I trace your ribcage with my finger imagining
a world of only men– a paradise of Adams.

IV. FIRST TIME

He wasn't you.
His body softer,
mouth smaller.

And I wasn't me.
Two bodies orbiting—
nothing more.

I came home.
Washed away his scent.
You smiled,

and we made love
like strangers,
our bodies reborn.

V. CONSEQUENCE

The dog won't lick your face when you come home
        from another man's bed (he doesn't like sharing).

VI. ONLINE

Adam sends you an electronic smile,
teeth glittering with pixels.
His digital avatar has only a cock,
a torso, no head, like some Greek
mythical creature rising from
technology's glistening rivers.

Adam is the first man. He's old,
and likes to compliment the boys,
expects "nothing" in return,
will pay for a trip to Europe,
tuition for college, drug money,
anything a twink might like.

Adam is 19, likes bareback sex
with strangers, thinks AIDS
was a bad 80s movie he slept
through, wants you to come in
using the key under the mat.
No speaking, just fucking.

Adam is married with a car-
seat in his SUV. His stomach
is pudgy, was once a six-pack,
once the star quarterback
of his high school team.
Now, he fucks like he's 15.

Adam is every man in our computer
file marked "dirty pictures."
Adam is you. Adam is me.

VII. THE DREAM

Last night I dreamt we flew to California
to get married like those same-sex couples
on the news channel vowing to love
each other forever, or until the angry church-
goers find a way to void that love. I dreamt
I wore white, not a gown, but flowing
and you wore a tux, the same one you once sang
foreign love songs in on an academic stage,
me in the audience applauding.

We were beautiful, in the dream,
with Hollywood tans and teeth that glowed
like television sets, but the plane crashed
before we ever made it to the West Coast,
(a bomb? God's wrath?—I don't know),
but there in singed clothes I cradled
your burnt body, wiped the ash from your
face, found your lips, and kissed them pink
again as you looked up and said, "paper burns,
means nothing." I laughed. The smoke
rose from our hair and curled above us.

VIII. CONSEQUENCE

Our sex life is wilder now, turned on by the boys
    we fuck (rebels in pink collared shirts).

IX. ONLINE

Electronic Adam says "you lookin'?"
I say our fig leaves are getting itchy.

You think yours is poison ivy,
but the Boy Scout in me knows better.

Adam will remove it anyway,
exposing your darkened thigh,

and off you'll go to his tree house,
your eyes burning brighter.

Leave the leaves to the trees,
I whisper as you come back

naked, beautiful, smelling of another
Adam, of another leaf.

X. JEALOUSY

We fight with passion now as if this could be the end
of us—together. Our slamming of doors echoes
louder, a pouring forth of emotion like a flood
that wipes all the sin away until we are nothing
but clean, naked bodies. Afterwards, you find me
in the bedroom full of empty threats, and we ask
the necessary questions (was it? was he?) and give
the necessary answers (of course not, no one is sexier
or more beautiful, I'll love you forever and ever,

amen).

XI. CONSEQUENCE

The possibility of falling in love with another increases
      (the risk we nonverbally agree to).

XII. ONLINE

Adam falls in love easily,
is jealous of you and me together,
angry, too, at our disregard

for convention. He longs
for an Adam of his own,
one to curl up on the couch with

watching TV, to cook dinner
for, to make love with in the dark.
He wants us to see the error

of our ways, to grovel
at the steps of monogamy,
to help keep his fantasy alive.

Adam is afraid of the rising
storm, of falling from grace,
of creating a new world.

XIII. A NEW WORLD

In the beginning there was Adam
        and Adam was lonely.
And God said, *I'll make you a companion,*
        a lover, a partner for all time.

There was a great tremble in Adam's
        flesh and from his rib sprung new life,
another man, an equal pairing.
        And Adam loved his Adam.

They shared secrets, sang love songs,
        nestled in the trees of paradise.
And God said, *it is good.*

And I say let us begin a new story,
        whisper our confessions to the rustle
of palm trees against bedroom windows,
        where we lay chest to chest,

body on body, just two Adams colliding
        in space, no longer alone,
no longer afraid of our mysterious planet.

ALLISON SHANE

boys who search for real life

Shane Allison has been called a fag, a nigger, and a genius. His poetry has graced the pages of *Mississippi Review*, *New Delta Review*, *Chiron Review*, *RFD*, *Spork*, *Velvet Mafia*, and many others. His first volume of poetry, *Slut Machine*, has been unleashed on the masses from Rebel Satori Press. He is a gay erotic anthologist at Cleis Press and is currently at work on a sex memoir and writing poems for a new volume.

KISS ME JOHN, BEFORE YOUR WIFE COMES HOME

Kiss me John, before your wife comes home.
Let's make love on a floor of pizza boxes.
Hands beneath your red shirt.
Come on baby give me something to remember you by.
Let's make love on a floor of empty pizza boxes,
Drink cream soda out of champagne glasses.
Come on baby give me something to remember you by
Before your wife gets off work.
Drink cream soda out of champagne glasses
As we sit eating Hungry Howies pizza on your ugly sofa.
Before your wife gets off work,
I want to feel your beard against my face
As we sit eating Hungry Howies pizza on your flowered sofa.
Fingers in your jungle of chest hair,
Your sand paper-beard against my face.
I want your pubes to tickle my nose
As fingers play in your jungle of chest hair.
I've waited to place myself between your ivory thighs,
Shorts down to pinkish ankles.
Black pubes tickle my nose.
I have waited to place myself between your ivory thighs
And suckle your meat during the director's cut of *Star Wars*
As black pubes tickle my nose.
Sink my teeth in your cheeks,
Suck your dick during the director's cut of *Star Wars*,
Taste your cream soda,
Sink my teeth in your cheeks,
Before your wife comes home.

CUTE BLACK JANITOR

Come here in your navy sweat shirt,
green pants around your pitch-black ankles.
Forget about the wife and kids and come to me.
Haven't we met,
haven't I seen you here before?
You're the cute black janitor
Messages about you are sketched in green
and yellow paint on the walls of stalls.
Where is that black dude with the uncut dick?
Gay janitors give the best head.
Look at me when I'm talking to you.
I want to blow you in the front seat
of your lime-green Cadillac.
Bend over.
I want to stuff your chocolate ass
like a Thanksgiving turkey.
Meet me on the first floor.
There's a hole more glorious
than drag queens to stuff your dick through.
You can wipe your cum on the sleeve
of my corduroy coat.
I write my phone number on two-ply tissue paper.
I stick it in your back pocket.
Here's my number, call me if you want to hang out,
drink a few beers and have your dick hummed on.
Four-eyed fat boy wants to
rim the black bubble butt
of a cute black janitor.

A DREAM

Used to
       wonder
              late at night

Boxers
           or
                          Briefs

           or

    just
    your
    naked
    ass

under
        JC Penney
                    sheets.

HIGH SCHOOL EPITHALAMION

Roivernon Adams proposes to Travis Asbell
Travis Asbell proposes to Scott Barber
Scott Barber proposes to Michael Brack
Michael Brack proposes to Ryan Bruce
Ryan Bruce proposes to John Brice
John Brice is marrying Lee Conner
Lee Conner is marrying Aaron Carroll
Aaron Carroll is marrying Jason Casseaux
Jason Casseaux just married David Chaffin
David Chaffin just married Michael Chapple
Michael Chapple just married Carlton Crawford
Carlton Crawford proposed to Joshua Cummings
But Joshua Cummings married Fred Davis
Fred Davis proposed to Shawn Davis
But Shawn Davis married Xavier Dempsy
Xavier Dempsy proposed to Dwayne Estelle
But Dwayne Estelle married James Fuse
James Fuse was engaged to Chris Gayre
Chris Garye was engaged to Shay Gibson
Shay Gibson was engaged to Darren Gibson
Darren Gibson was engaged to Shawn Gregg
Shawn Gregg eloped with Brian Gurr
Brian Gurr eloped with Michael Hardy
Michael Hardy ran away with Grady Harper
Grady Harper ran away with Michael Harris
Michael Harris ran away with Moise Harris
Moise Harris was married to Andy Harrison
Andy Harrison was married to Eric Hatcher
Eric Hatcher was married to Richard Herring
Richard Herring said yes to Brandon Houston
Brandon Houston said yes to David Hove
David Hove said yes to Danny James
Danny James said yes to Rashaan Jones
Rashaan Jones proposed to Travis Jones
Travis Jones proposed to Scott Joyner
Scott Joyner proposed to Chad Keen
Chad Keen proposed to John Keillor
John Keillor eloped with Brian Kelly
Brian Kelly eloped with Clint Kinsey
Clint Kinsey eloped with Brent LaBounty
Brent LaBounty ran away with Richard Langly

Richard Langly ran away with Dwayne Lawrence
Dwayne Lawrence ran away with Abe Lerner
Abe Lerner used to be married to Richard Lollie
Richard Lollie used to be married to Thomas Migut
Thomas Migut used to be married to Brian Miller
Brian Miller used to be married to Ed Mock
Ed Mock used to be married to David Moore
David Moore used to be married to Fred Nichols
Fred Nichols is engaged to Shawn O'shields
Shawn O'shields is engaged to Willie Parker
Willie Parker is engaged to Bryan Reed
Bryan Reed ran off with Cleveland Richardson
Cleveland Richardson ran off with Jason Rowland
Jason Rowland ran off with Andy Salley
Andy Salley ran off with David Simmons
David Simmons just married Myron Steen
Myron Steen just married Alvin Tabanguil
Alvin Tabanguil just married Ed Thompson
Ed Thompson proposed to Samuel Towels
Samuel Towels proposed to Anthony Whitehead
Anthony Whitehead proposed to Leroy Williams
Leroy Williams proposed to Titus Williams
But Titus Williams married Russell Wilson

HE'S A SLUT

a dick sucking scumbag
who lets any man treat his mouth
like a public toilet.
His saliva dries on my cock.
Finger inserted in virgin core wedding ring deep.
He's a stall stalking slum lord
who preys on blond haired frat boys.
Smothers his face in strangling pubes.
He doesn't mind a bubble butt nesting on his face.
He likes a mouth full of shit,
piss splashing against the wall of his back.
He's a dirty old man.
A pervert praying on the blood
of boys who search for real life
adventures of true love.

DRAMA QUEEN
In response to Vytautas Pliura's poem, My Mother is Jean Harlow

Your mama might be Jean Harlow but my mama is Joan Crawford.
She never beat me with wire hangers.
She tore my ass up with
leather belts and bedroom shoes.
Instead of scrubbing the bathroom floor with Dutchman cleanser,
I had to clean out the garage, soak her teeth in Fixodent.
I helped her to the toilet after she went to the
doctor to have her bunions removed.
She never fed me milk and cookies after school.
She didn't bake cakes or knit sweaters for me.
The sweet potato pies, the golden brown turkey
were store-bought from Publix.
My mama was never into PTA meetings or throwing Tupperware parties.
She used to deliver telephone books door to door.
She never came to see me play a black Santa Claus
in my third grade Christmas play.
My mama is Cleopatra Jones with AK-47's and grenades
in the glove compartment of her Monte Carlo.
Your mama might be a Blonde Bombshell,
but my mama got hot curls her hair.
She greases it with hair mayonnaise
My brother miscarried in her womb.
Til this day, I don't know where the hell he's buried.
So what if you grew up on a farm churning buttermilk,
stepping in Angus shit? I went to a high school where the principal said
I exposed my dick to some supposed white girl.
Her name was privileged information.
Who cares if your mother is Jean Harlow?
My mama is Wonder Woman catching missiles
like Frisbees, bending crowbars in her hands.
She works undercover at Radiology Associates
emptying garbage cans filled with hazardous waste.
She brings home greasy smothered chicken on Styrofoam plates.
She's Weezie Jefferson before getting a piece of the pie
on the Upper East Side.
Does Jean Harlow cook pig's feet?
Whip you up a mess of mustard greens, Jiffy mix cornbread?
Does she wash shit out of your underpants or is she too busy
playing a damsel in distress, draped over some man's arms like a bath towel.

Your movie-star mama might smell like Chanel No. 5,
but my mama smells like raspberry-scented shower gel.
So, your mother's Jean Harlow? If she's so famous,
then she won't mind if we invite a few friends
over to her place for a pool party.
View a couple of her old pictures that made her a star.
You think Jean can lend me a couple of bucks
to pay back my student loans?

I THINK YOU SHOULD KNOW

Think you should know that it's 3 a.m. and I haven't jacked off all day.
Think you should know that I occupy a double room on 84 William St.
    All to myself.
Think you should know that when my Korean roommates
    Are next door in the double loft area sound asleep,
    I like to dance naked to George Michael songs.
Think you should know that right now, right this minute,
    I'm lying in a lower bunk with my *Fruit of the Looms*
    Up around my ankles. I think it's important to let you know
    My legs are spread apart like knitting needles hiked above me.
Think you should know that I'm caressing my balls.
    I'm not sure, but I think cum is swirling around in my ball sac.
Think you need to know that as I lie here exploring myself with fingers,
    I can feel tiny hairs in the dark honey comb of my butt.
Think you should know that my dick beats against my belly.
Think you should be aware that my feet are touching the railings
    At the bottom of my top bunk.
Think you should know that my butthole has grown wet
    Thinking about your dick at my anus.
Just think you should be aware that I'm tight down there.
Think you should know that I'm playing with myself
    On these navy-blue bed sheets.
Just want you to know that I'm thinking of you standing
    Naked at my face.
Think you should know that there's nothing I find cuter
    Than a dick with foreskin, baby.
    Central air-conditioning blows up my ass.
I just want you to know that I've been thinking lately,
    About your Carolina cock.
Think you should know that I worship dicks with dickcheese.
    Did you know that I have yet to discover any Big Apple dick?
I think you need to know that if I don't get some dick pretty soon,
    I'm going to be one more pissed off fag.
Just want you to know that if I don't get laid before I die,
    I'm going to be a pissed off queer angel. A cock ring for a halo.
Think you should be aware that the naked photos are in the mail.
Think you should know that I wait for yours just the same.
Think you should know that I stuck my finger up my butt
    And took a whiff of the inner me.
I think you should know that men hold hands here.
I think you should know that a Latino man got beat in the head

    For being a queen in Queens.
I think you should know I saw a bald guy with a high-tight ass
    Walking down 13th St.
Think you should know that jacking off
    Only goes so far with me before I start grabbing the random asses
    Of men, randomly.
Think you should know that the glory holes here are as big as watermelons.
I think you should know that I wish you were here.
I think you should know I'm holding a special place
    For you in my tawdry ass, so when you come,
      I'll be naked and waiting.
Think you should know that I'm a virgin.

HITTINGER
MATTHEW

this tesseract we make

Matthew Hittinger is the author of the chapbooks *Pear Slip* (Spire Press, 2007), winner of the Spire 2006 Chapbook Award, *Narcissus Resists* (GOSS183/MiPOesias, 2009), and *Platos de Sal* (Seven Kitchens Press, 2009). His work has appeared in many journals and the anthologies *Best New Poets 2005* and *Ganymede Poets, One.* Matthew lives and works in New York City.

www.matthewhittinger.com

INTERVIEW WITH MS. HORTENSE CORPULENCE
AFTER HER FINAL ATLANTIS CRUISE LINE PERFORMANCE

Gurl, today I received a three-fold post-
    card from *Playboy*. Lord
knows how they found Ms. Hortense on this cruise
    ship but I suspect
an agenda, a recruitment effort
    if there ever was
one. That buxom, flaxen, half-human, half-
    silicone wo-man
clearly plugs a skinthetic life. Such lips
    and hips and tits—just
think of the woman I could become snug
    in a double D
cup. Shit of course six inch stilettos cramp
    the feet but when you
are as short as me honey you need all
    the height you can get.

Need I remind you in the years before
    RuPaul's Drag Race—when
Ongina stomped into our hearts, Nina
    Flowers bent gender,
spanked it, and Pandora Boxx was robbed her
    win— outside of balls
when I reigned supreme, Mother of the House
    of Corpulence, one
had to compete on Jenny Jones—better
    yet, Ricki Lake—grace
a stage junk tucked and taped in a low-cut
    one-piece, sequined high-
slit, peacock boa and talent! Now I'm
    not one to throw shade
but look out skanks, listen to this diva
    work and turn it out:

These hips, these hips need
mambo and flamenco as they swivel
    and slip, as they slink
through tight places. Try to grip these hips; they
rip with volt. Try to ride these hips, they buck
    wi-ld as a horse.

> *These hips, these hips will*
> *have you on your knees, will roll to tease; they'll*
> >   *zip you down and whip*
> *a rhythm close to ecs-ta-sy; en-trance,*
> *they'll trance, put a spell on a man, silence*
> >   *his lips with one dip.*

But who am I kidding, not those men, oh
>   no. That studio
audience is gonna whoop and hollar;
>   the fools'll vote all
the small-breasted, natural-born girls "men."
>   Sorry ladies, chop
chop. And when the women out there vote my
>   rivals "men" too, I
know I'll have a chance. You ladies make me
>   feel, *yes, you make me*
feel a one hundred percent, genuine
>   *wo-man.* Boy-o, look
at Miss Thang. Come meet me on the street—would
>   you think twice? Picture
your nose buried deep in my cleavage. They're
>   real baby, not beat.

Now I'm no painted puppet in a nymph's
>   attire. Come over
here, honey. Let me slip off my scarf, look
>   at the apple stuck
in my throat. Let me tip my hat, expose
>   my *umbrella, el-*
la, ella's underside, bare the backside
>   of my belt. Will you
read one hundred percent sizzling, sexy
>   man? Sugar, don't gag.
I'm every woman and can read your
>   *thoughts* : "She was the real
deal, yes, the hottest thang here." Fierce, I know.
>   Just goes to show : when
it's ovah, one's never too short—*ha ha!*
>   to be a drag queen.

VERTEX

Ocher-veined tiles diamond my mind,
a Sierpinski carpet : white rhombs petal-

scattered, Swarovski chandelier light
fake like so much here : Ionic column

spiral pre-recorded, no harmonics
under this dome, this temple to the God

of product, Goddess of purchase. You find
me here, red arch framed, lost in espresso

bar, in escalator slide. You approach :
like a hawk spots prey, an insect toward light,

the angle formed between you and me, pitch
of the spiral the path you take. I tense.

Wrought iron chair feet scrape. I mistake you.
Your eyes smile brighter than Nordstrom's sign.

People pass by like bees, pocket pollen,
enter stores which are nothing more than cells,

honey-filled hexagons. You sit. My leg
twitches knee nudged into thigh. I bookmark

my page, leave lilacs in New York for King
of Prussia's crosses, its cubes unfolded.

You risk a hand drop, run a dark fold formed
by my bent crossed knee under fingernail,

accentuate the crease. My thigh warms your
hand. This tesseract we make : I enter

you, you enter me and the cube breaks all
endless spiral: yellow light from a bent

sun flower head, the tropical storm's arms,
its silent eye : we are each two arms in this

four-armed Milky Way, and while I small talk
the office, orange sweater on a lifeless

mannequin, the lack of size 29 waist
pants, a point beneath my voice, behind your

eyes enters the mind's chambered nautilus.
We rise, two temples of tendon and bone,

blend into the dark floor, into the cast
light : the moment telegraphed *stop* we go.

MOVIE SHOOT AT THE EMPIRE HOTEL

The day I left New York a mass
    of teenage extras lined
either side of the revolving doors, side-walk
    narrowed to an aisle.

            The doorman
        apologized as we waited
                in the vaulted lobby for the cameras
to finish rolling and when the Director yelled
                cut
            they let me leave.

    I dislodged
sunglasses from my hair, the teens
        tinted orange as, stoic, they
            barely parted. All girls,
        many seemed too
old for tight clothes, many
        too young for made-
           up faces as they waited for the next
        take. I waited out

of the way for a cab. The Director
    tried the scene again : non-
descript caucasian actor leaves the glass
    doors, eyes hidden behind
        sunglasses, yet now the mob
            screams and claws
        through black body-

        guards as they escort the actor
into an SUV. Of course editing will make John
    Doe into a sex symbol.

            The light turns red
    at the block's end, and I catch
        the cabbie glance at me as I glance
at the hotel, the crowd, the SUV.
            His right eye draws
        a line to my right.

SKIN GAME

Leopard tiger zebra / prints store fronts all drape
and cinch such warmth such style / those mannequins *skin is*

*in start and end with skin / when energy peters
out skin still wins* fashion / turns the animal trend

sends last season to task / masked cannibals ask *will
wearing others' flimsy / skins still be in once flayed*

fur flies imagine if / you are what you eat are
you what you wear cheat death / dare to hide in hide *hard*

*plastic pallid valid / word beneath the makeup
mask the dress and pearls suit / and tie the skins in which*

*we die and lie about / our birth beyond wrinkles
beyond surface beyond / scars pocks and spots* patterns

won't lie camouflage must / swap its basic colors
to survive or else face / sabotage cleave *why not*

simply lie and foreign / forces colonize *lie
in original skin* / anti-bodies bargain

think of what skin bars gains / infection admission
relation *is that such / a sin* nation-building

taken to a whole new / win skin the skin *skin is
skin and never nothing / always something more so*

skinthetic stratified / *so skintastic* forget
muscle and fat feel bronze / or copper metallic

names epidermis turned / to fool's gold *time to slip*
hold the melanoma / alchemies high and *time*

to shift fight the rich conned / out of fudge vanilla
mocha the names we make / to differentiate

to fake power purpose / *to put the in in skin*
joined so close what's to keep / skin A from B porous

chorus Latinize derm's / epithelial fun
lined inside out with pelt / and felt pelt the felt stoned

secrets break our hold we / coat the body's fire
in latex coats *other* / *desire* cavity

organ lubed we slip in / to ourselves rim and delve
rhyme skin with skin and what / sound do you get swindled

KEYSTONE EFFECT: POLE STEEPLE

One Saturday we drove to Pine Grove Furnace
past fields globbed gold a thick impasto autumn
caught in an angle of light lodged like his hand
       in my unzipped pants.

Car parked at lake edge we stalked each other
with arms full of leaves something blossoming
under those crisp red edges smell of dried
       chlorophyll heavy in the air.

The trail punctuated with boulders thick roots
winded us; a family in matching parkas hikers
with heavy wool socks a class from the college
       dotted the blotchy rock.

Against azure backdrop from base to top Pole
Steeple vibrated; he dropped my hand found
foot holds up edifices past a perched dog ward
       of some unseen master.

At Steeple top the wind gained body and voice
caressed rock appendages worried away edges;
we skirted the crowd stole kisses in crevices
       precipice inches away.

His kisses blinded like the gold slit of the lake
our thirst quickened by the wind. We kept warm
in each other's pockets circled round peak back
       past a charred fire spot.

We paused here, before singled-out trees branded
with red trail markers; a plaque's inset letters
read *Appalachian Trail* that stretch that journey
       from Maine to Georgia.

All paths have those isolate places perfect for two
to perch one on his knees one part of an ecstasy
filtered through shrubby bramble shadows alert
       to trouble every coming.

ONE DAY HOMO

appeared the beige plaster
flaked off the wall where the gray

marker amended the black spray
paint Mo there for months

a pre-teen's tag the Ho added
overnight greeting or threat

or the games of the adolescent
my bedroom window view

A BUS JOURNEYS WEST

A Haitian couple, a Jamaican chef
    a Puerto Rican

student studying for her English test
    wait in the empty

Port Authority terminal. An old
    Polish man shuffles

by with a sandwich, half-shouts *This the line?*
    grumbles under his

breath as he backtracks. The bus driver takes
    our tickets, a pink

light enriches his caramel skin, thin
    smile, wrinkles kiss

his eye and lip corners, his furrowed brow.
    We depart, couple

and chef by the bathroom, the girl somewhere
    center, the old man

behind the driver and since traffic bound
    for Lincoln Tunnel

creeps even slower these days, each in turn
    has a chance to see

the white balloon caught in the barbed wire
    of the Croatian

Catholic Church before the slight downward
    slope, orange tunnel lights

doubled in windows, spectacles, tiled walls,
    each vehicle crowned

by yellow lines, two lanes headed under
    and out, Jersey's air

queer, the New York sky-line behind, more lights
    on its streets, in dark

building silhouettes than people : five, ten,
    fifteen to twenty

for every man, every woman or two
    beams, twins containing

thousands pressed against clouds that drift broken
    into strata, high

widened disseminating touch not god
    disappeared into

atmosphere, not heaven, not universe,
    they plummet and fall

to the ground night after night, doused. New York
    recedes, the rusty

clouds our only reminder. The chef sips
    beer wrapped in a brown

bag, cracks two peanut shells and offers them
    "*Eskize*, peanut?"

to the couple nestled in, *"Mèsi plen,"*
    from the husband. "D-

anyen. Ya smell smoke?" And the intercom
    crackles: *Now I know*

nobody's smokin' on my bus. A pause
    as we catch a whiff

of nicotine, scan the aisles for smoke.
    Sir, I suggest you

come outta that bathroom. A full minute
    passes. *Sir, if you*

don't come out I will call the cops. The door
        swings open, old man

coughs, holds the aisle seat tops to steady
        himself. "Why ya tek

so long?" asks the chef. The old man ignores
        him, the driver goes

on : *I'm tired of people breakin' the rules
        on this bus. Got kids*

*sellin' drugs, fights breakin' out, you people
        smokin' up. I won't*

*stand for it. Not on my bus. You go ride
        somebody else's*

*bus if you wanna do that shit. What'd you
        say? Don't you cuss me*

out. Old man switches from Polish curses
        to English ones. *Don't*

think I won't call the cops. At our next stop,
        an empty parking

lot, five squad cars surround us, red and blue
        lights flash and transform

the bus into a dance club. "Well Lawd haw
        mercy, would ya look

pon dat now." The police escort him, one
        stays, asks *This guy been*

causin' you all trouble? The student laughs
        "Officer, he stole

my purse!" and clutches her English grammar
        book. A lone chuckle

rises from the Haitian man : *Ravet pa
    janm gen rezon*

devan poul! His wife interprets : "Roaches
    are never right when

facing chickens." Our driver, weary with
    broken rules, backtalk,

chortles in relief? At expense? *Well, I
    have nothing against

smokers, just as long as they don't do it
    on my bus.* One laugh

joins another and soon the laughter spreads,
    the moment light, full

of light from ten reading lamps, five police
    cars, the moon. *You all

have good nights now*, wishes the officer
    and then we drive on,

one less but still divided, the nations
    of a trip headed

West, away from the city we must pass,
    the city where we

split, peanut shells cracked, sandwich crust littered,
    grammar choked and dust.

DILLARD
GAVIN

better'n the best sex

Gavin Geoffrey Dillard has published ten collections of verse, two anthologies, and his infamous Hollywood tell-all, *IN THE FLESH: Undressing for Success*. Also known as "the Naked Poet," his poems have been recorded by James Earl Jones and published in myriad periodicals. Gavin has written lyrics with and for such luminaries as Sam Harris, Jake Heggie, Peter Allen, Chanticleer, and Disney Studios; his classical art songs have been featured at Lincoln Center; he has written comedy with and for Dolly Parton, Joan Rivers, Peggy Lee, Vincent Price, and Lily Tomlin. His current musical, *BARK!*, is playing worldwide, and two new musicals, *OMFG!!!* and *The Naked Poet*, premiere in 2011 in San Francisco and Los Angeles, respectively.

(ADVICE TO A YOUNG SERB)

Love requires no opinion. Love requires no belief. It doesn't take work and it doesn't take conflict;

Love is what is when you stop fighting. It is the simplest common denominator.

Most people only smell it now and then around the corner, they never get a bite;

But it is inside you, as a very subtle feeling. And it is far more precious than any relationship.

Generally speaking you have to feel the love within you first before you can sense it elsewhere, unless you have the great fortune to encounter a saint, one who knows love and can give without requiring back;

Love doesn't make the world a good or happy place, necessarily, but it makes it worth living, and it makes it make sense. With love one can relax and stop fighting, because you are always already home.

Romance is another matter altogether!

DECEMBER 18, 2009

Lost for hours, we ended up spaing in Hot Springs, NC;
26 degrees out, we screamed ourselves dressed, huddled long against the
 bon fire flames, raced to the frigid Volvo;
berry cobbler and hot ciders at the Bacchus Bistro in Marshall,
 then closed (midnight) the Chocolate Lounge in Asheville;
your ass around my finger, it was the first time you quit yammering all
 day; finally kissing goodnight, I left no questions in your mouth.

APHORISMS

-1-

I'm too much of an aesthetic to be an ascetic;
and besides, I don't plan to come back here again,
so I don't want to miss anything this time around.

APHORISMS

-2-

 I was commenting to the farmer I buy fresh goat milk from how
positively sweet and floral is his (the goats') milk,
 he explained that the key is in not having a male goat even anywhere
on the property, that billies pee on their own beards and just a
 kiss through a fence is enough to infect the nannies' milk;
I casually mentioned that I have known many a Billy who
 did just that, and though it rarely prevented me from
kissing them, more than once was the milk sour before it
 ever made it to my table.

APHORISMS

-3-

In a stiff white-cotton bed,
awaiting the removal of a derelict
organ, I cannot help but
wonder in whose garden the
moon now sits.

APHORISMS

-4-

Another rude scar left by a
bepassioned lover in the
 middle of the night—
now my appendix is gone
 and so is Dr Shikibu.

APHORISMS

-5-

You may well be envious of my world—
and right you would be to be so—for
      everything in it is perfect:
the sound of the rain dripping from eaves onto
      the gingers and ape leaves,
three exquisite kittens who want my undivided
      attention at all times;
the constant cups of genmaicha and
      barley coffee,
the feel of my testicles through flannel pajamas,
books I write almost daily that will
      never be published;
a wooden begging bowl from my first Guru which
      always contains nothing,
apples and goat cheese, Scottish shortbread with
      chewy pieces of ginger inside,
green papaya which, when steamed, tastes like
      the inside of broccoli stalks;
incense sticks which burn away to smell like the
      ashes of forgotten lovers,
a leak in the roof as predictable as religion,
buffalo horn earrings that have ceased to cause my
      earlobes to bleed;
geckoes in the corners that sound like
      Chinese merchants,
that I am no longer afraid to use the word
      God—that I can see
God in all the minutiae of creation and
      fabrication; that I can
touch anything now—eat, breathe, urinate—and
      know that it is sacred.

APHORISMS

-6-

No more love letters,
at this age I get reminders from my
 doctor;
but what does he know, he's living in a
 dream world of organs and
pathogens—
 while I, with bursting heart, listen to my
Beloved whisper from
 river, stone and tree …

APHORISMS

-7-

What's the point of sexual liberation,
if only to become a slave to one's own desires?

APHORISMS

-8-

"Safe sex" is an oxymoron;
why on earth would anyone want *safe* sex?
 condoms are for accountants and real estate sissies,
condoms and for bozos and bankers;
 real men don't drink pharmaceutical cocktails,
real men drink acid coffee with spit in it,
 real men wear barbed wire belts;
and as for love … puleeze, if it doesn't kill you,
 if it doesn't rip your ass open and leave you drowned in a
pool of sperm and blood …
 well, then what's the fucking point?

APHORISMS

-9-

Ecstatic union,
better'n chocolate, better'n espresso;
ecstatic union,
better'n the best sex, better'n winning the Lotto;
the face of God
obliterates all others;
brave men cower, strong men crumble,
the wise are speechless,
and no one comes out alive.

APHORISMS

-10-

I have no interest in anyone who has sex with their mind;
if I am going to mate, it will be with a tree:
 something with its roots in the earth and its
arms in the air, something that doesn't flee from storms or
 cower in the dark,
something that doesn't fret about a changing season or
 bemoan the loss of a mere limb;
something that can bend and break and continually
 reach for the sun and stars,
something that will feed me when the days of summer
 have passed.

SUBMIT TO ASSARACUS

The mission of Sibling Rivalry Press is to develop, publish, and promote outlaw artistic talent—those projects which inspire people to read, challenge, and ponder the complexities of life in dark rooms, under blankets by cell-phone illumination, in the backseats of cars, and on spring-day park benches next to people reading Plath and Whitman. We encourage submissions to *Assaracus* by gay male poets of any age, regardless of background, education, or level of publication experience. For more information, visit us online.

www.siblingrivalrypress.com

ALSO FROM SIBLING RIVALRY PRESS

***Burnings* by Ocean Vuong.** Says Roger Bonair-Agard, two time National Slam Champion and author of *Tarnish and Masquerade*: "These poems shatter us detail by detail because Ocean leaves nothing unturned, because every lived thing in his poems demands to be fed by you; to nourish you in turn. You will not leave these poems dissatisfied. They will fill you utterly."

***My Life as Adam* by Bryan Borland.** From Grady Harp, *Poets & Artists* Magazine: "'You have to have been there…' No, this insensitive statement regarding whether or not the reader can or would understand the depth of feeling of a journeyman is shattered in Bryan Borland's intensely honest and painfully lovely book of poems. Bryan enters his world as a nascent, ambiguous *Adam* and returns at the end a fully developed *Man*."

Fag Hag: A Scandalous Chapbook of Fabulously-Codependent Poetry. Poets come together to take on that mythological creature known as the fag hag—with humor, wit, and unfulfilled desire.

Ganymede Unfinished. John Stahle and *Ganymede* changed the face of gay publishing and introduced the world to the next generation of queer poets, writers, and artists. Though John died in April of 2010, his legacy is evident in this 300-plus page, 6x9 perfectly-bound journal published in his honor.

www.siblingrivalrypress.com

Lightning Source UK Ltd.
Milton Keynes UK
UKOW051234080812
197228UK00001B/262/P